PowerKids Readers:

My Library of Holidays™

May Harte

The Rosen Publishing Group's
PowerKids Press™
New York

Published in 2004 by The Rosen Publishing Group, Inc.
29 East 21st Street, New York, NY 10010

First Edition

Book Design: Michael J. Caroleo

Photo Credits: Cover and pp. 11, 22 (harvest) © Jose Luis Pelaez, Inc./CORBIS; p. 5 © Lake County Museum/CORBIS; pp. 7, 9, 13, 22 (Native Americans and Pilgrims) © Bettmann/CORBIS; p. 15 © Ariel Skelley/CORBIS; p. 17 © Rick Barrentine/CORBIS; p. 19 © Royalty-Free/CORBIS; pp. 21, 22 (parade) © Kelly-Mooney Photography/CORBIS; p. 22 (cranberry sauce) © Rick Barrentine/CORBIS.

Harte, May
Thanksgiving / May Harte.
p. cm. – (My library of holidays)
Includes bibliographical references and index.
Summary: This book explains the American history that led to the observance of our Thanksgiving and describes how our holiday is celebrated.
ISBN 1-4042-2527-7 (lib.)
1. Thanksgiving   [1. Thanksgiving   2. Holidays] I. Title   II. Series
    2004   2003-009217
394.2649–dc21

Manufactured in the United States of America

Contents

Thanksgiving is an American holiday. Do you know when Thanksgiving began?

Thanksgiving Day

GREETINGS.

James Brundage

Design Copyright 1910 by Francis Brundage.

5

In 1620, a group of people called the Pilgrims came to America from Europe. They came to find a better life in America.

The Pilgrims came on a boat called the *Mayflower*.

The Pilgrims found it hard to grow food during their first year in America. In the second year they were able to grow a harvest of good food.

In 1621, the Pilgrims had the first Thanksgiving. They gave thanks with the Native Americans who had helped them to grow the food.

Today, American families have Thanksgiving on the fourth Thursday of November every year.

15

People eat a lot of good food at Thanksgiving. Many families eat turkey and cranberry sauce.

People eat pumpkin pie, too.

19

Many people go to Thanksgiving Day parades. What do you do on Thanksgiving?

21

Words to Know

cranberry sauce

harvest

Native
Americans

parade

Pilgrims

Here are more books to read about Thanksgiving:

Countdown to Thanksgiving
by Jodi Huelin, Keiko Motoyama (Illustrator)
Penguin Putnam Books for Young Readers

If You Were at the First Thanksgiving
by Anne Kamma, Bert Dodson (Illustrator)
Scholastic, Inc.

The Thanksgiving Story
by Alice Dalgliesh, Helen Sewell (Illustrator)
Simon & Schuster Children's

Due to the changing nature of Internet links, PowerKids Press has developed an online list of Web sites related to the subject of this book. This site is updated regularly. Please use this link to access the list:

www.powerkidslinks.com/mlholi/thank/

Index

C
cranberry sauce, 16

F
food, 10, 16

H
harvest, 10, 12
holiday, 4
M
Mayflower, 8

N
Native Americans, 12

P
parades, 20
Pilgrims, 6, 8, 10, 12
pumpkin pie, 18

Word Count: 141

Note to Parents, Teachers, and Librarians

PowerKids Readers are specially designed to help emergent and beginning readers build their skills in reading for information. Simple vocabulary and concepts are paired with real-life photographs or stunning, detailed images from the natural world. Readers will respond to written language by linking meaning with their own everyday experiences and observations. Sentences are short and simple, employing a basic vocabulary of sight words, as well as new words that describe objects or processes that take place in the natural world. Large type, clean design, and photographs corresponding directly to the text all help children to decipher meaning. Features such as a contents page, picture glossary, and index help children to get the most out of PowerKids Readers. They also introduce children to the basic elements of a book, which they will encounter in their future reading experiences. Lists of related books and Web sites encourage kids to explore other sources and to continue the process of learning.